Keeping fish

David Cook

Illustrated by
Jim Channell and Gary Hincks

SCIMITAR 57-59 Long Acre, London WC2E 9JL

Keeping an aquarium

It was the Chinese who first had the idea of keeping fish as pets. Over a thousand years ago, they kept goldfish in basins hollowed out of blocks of stone. Their idea caught on. Today, fish keeping is a very popular hobby – not surprisingly, for managing an aquarium is not difficult. The results can often be spectacularly beautiful.

Fish make excellent pets. They are clean and don't smell unless there is something wrong with them. You don't have to take them for walks and you can even leave them for up to three weeks at a time.

Doctors and dentists often have aquaria in their waiting-rooms. Looking at the fish helps nervous patients to relax.

A coldwater aquarium is the simplest. You need only basic equipment – a covered tank, a filter and an aerator. However, the range of coldwater fish is small. Also, coldwater fish need plenty of oxygen and swimming space. You can keep only a few in a small tank.

Coldwater aquarium

There are three kinds of aquaria – cold freshwater, tropical freshwater, and seawater. Coldwater aquaria are the simplest to set up but tropical tanks are far more colourful. If you want to keep tropical fish you will need some rather expensive equipment to heat the water and keep it at the right temperature. But apart from the expense of setting up, they cost no more to keep than coldwater fish.

Seawater aquaria are hard to keep and unsuitable for beginners. This book only deals with coldwater and tropical aquaria.

If you enjoy keeping fish, and even want to breed them, you would do well to join an aquarium club. There, experts can help you.

In a tropical aquarium you will need a heater, and a thermometer, as well as the equipment used in a coldwater tank. As tropical fish are quite small (often only 4-5cm long) you can keep a good number together. There is a wide range of fish to choose from.

Tropical aquarium

What every fish needs

If fish are to live happily in captivity they must be properly cared for. First, you need a suitable tank. Choose one with a large surface area so that plenty of air can reach the water. Never keep fish in bowls.

When picking a tank, remember that it will be very heavy when filled with water. It must have a strong support so you may have to buy a special stand. A good size tank for a beginner is about 60cm x 30cm x 38cm. It will weigh about 100kg when full and can hold either four 8cm Goldfish or about 18 tropical fish of 4-5cms.

You will need gravel at the bottom of the tank in which to grow plants. Larger rocks are attractive too. They provide shelter for fish. Not all are suitable so ask an expert which ones to put in. The water must be heated to about 24°C for most species of tropical fish. For coldwater ones, the water should be at room temperature.

Plants help in a small way to restore the balance of oxygen and carbon dioxide in the water (below). Given plenty of light, plants take in carbon dioxide from the water and give off oxygen. Fish, on the other hand, breathe oxygen in and carbon dioxide out.

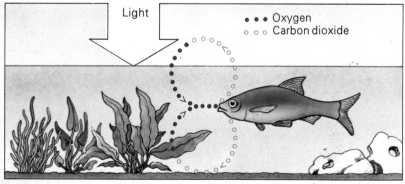

Light

● ● ● Oxygen
○ ○ ○ Carbon dioxide

Like all animals, fish must breathe. But instead of having lungs like land animals, they have gills. They take in oxygen from the water and breathe out carbon dioxide.

Never overcrowd your tank with fish or there won't be enough oxygen for them all. With too little, fish do not grow healthily. As conditions get worse, they will come to the surface gasping for air. If there still isn't enough oxygen in the water, they will very soon die.

Most of the oxygen in water is drawn from the air. A large surface area in the tank means that plenty of oxygen can reach the water. Here too, carbon dioxide breathed out by the fish escapes back into the air.

An aerator makes sure there is enough oxygen in the water by pumping a constant stream of air through it. It also disturbs the surface which helps the exchange of oxygen and carbon dioxide.

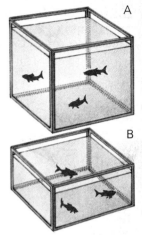

How many fish you can keep depends on a tank's surface area – not its depth. Tank A can hold no more fish than Tank B.

Allow 20 sq. cm of surface water for every centimetre of coldwater fish ; 8 sq. cm of surface for every centimetre of tropical fish. (right). Don't include the fish's tail in your measurements and remember, fish grow ! A tropical tank must also be deep enough to let plants grow properly.

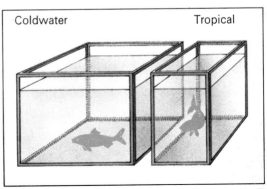

Coldwater   Tropical

Aquarium equipment

There are two kinds of filter – biological and mechanical. Biological ones (above) lie under the gravel. Mechanical ones look like small plastic boxes and are attached to the outside of the tank or put in an inside corner.

A cover for your tank is a must. It not only keeps dust out and cuts down loss of water by evaporation, it also keeps fish in. Many fish can jump. If not restrained, they may launch themselves out onto your living-room carpet. The cover should fit loosely to allow air in and out freely.

Light is important, especially in tropical aquaria where it shows off your fish well and makes plants flourish. A 60cm x 30cm x 38cm tropical tank should have two 40 watt bulbs. A coldwater tank of the same size needs two 25 watt bulbs. They should be kept on for about ten hours a day.

A well kept tank not overstocked with fish shouldn't need an aerator; but they are useful. They ensure there's plenty of air and an even temperature throughout the tank. A filter, to clean the water, can be attached to the aerator. Never use an aerator as an excuse to overcrowd your tank.

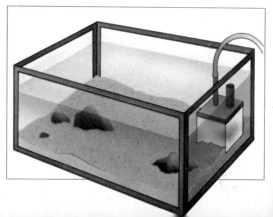

Properly kept aquaria are light, clean and well aerated. This means having lighting and an aerator and filter system. A tropical aquarium also needs a heater with a thermostat control that keeps the temperature correct automatically. A thermometer to check the temperature is essential ; it is not unknown for thermostats to go wrong ! Keeping the tank clean is most important. You will sometimes need a siphon or dip tube to remove any waste the filter cannot cope with or food you may have spilt. Feeding rings keep food in one place, so fish know where to look for it and there is less chance of it falling to the bottom uneaten. Nets are important for catching fish without hurting them or up-rooting the plants. You need two – one to drive the fish into the other. Use a scraper to clean algae off the glass.

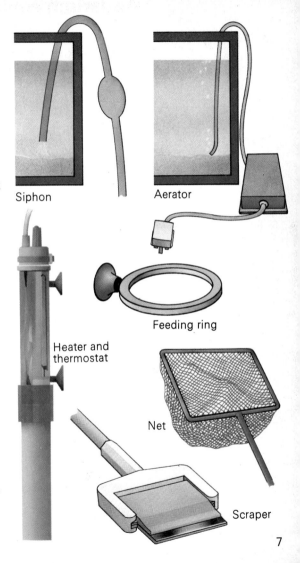

Siphon

Aerator

Feeding ring

Heater and thermostat

Net

Scraper

7

Setting up

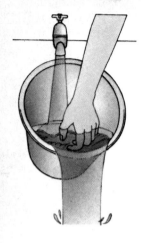

Dirty gravel causes problems in a tank. Rinse the gravel thoroughly, a little at a time, in a clean bucket.

Place your tank in a bright spot but out of direct sunlight. Avoid anything that may drastically change the water temperature, like open windows or radiators. Wash the tank in lukewarm water before filling it. Never use detergents or bleach.

If you are not using a biological filter put clean gravel in the tank first. Slope it higher at the back and low in front so you can see clearly into the aquarium. This also helps keep the tank clean. Sediment will slip down to the bottom of the slope where you can easily siphon it off.

When putting in rocks and plants remember that you must be able to see into the tank. You also want it to look beautiful. So arrange plants round the back and sides of the aquarium with the tall ones behind the short ones. Leave the front fairly clear. Try and make an attractive background for your fish.

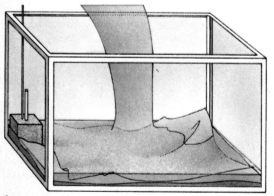

Put the clean gravel in your tank sloping it higher at the back and low at the front. Fill the tank half full of water pouring it gently over a plate or a sheet of paper (left), so it does not disturb the gravel. It is easier to put in the plants when the tank is half full than when it is empty.

Be careful with water and electricity – the combination can be lethal. So get help in setting up the equipment and make sure it's protected from splashes.

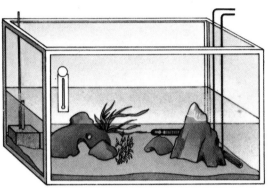

When the tank is half full of water put in the rocks and plants. Keep the front of the tank clear or you won't be able to see the fish. When setting up the mechanical equipment, put the heater in a back corner of the tank. Always carefully follow the instructions given by the manufacturer.

Fill the tank with water and put on the cover. Switch on the equipment and leave the tank to settle for two or three days before putting in any fish. This gives the plants time to start to root, lets the water become cleaner and allows you to check that the equipment is working.

Water plants

Rooted plants (R) should be planted one by one in the gravel at the bottom of the tank.

An aquarium without plants would be very dull. But plants are useful as well as pretty. They provide the fish with natural surroundings and give them shade and shelter when they want to hide.

One kind of plant life you won't be able to avoid is algae. It collects on the glass and will need scraping off. Algae may turn the water green. If this happens, reduce the amount of light for a week or so. A Sucking Loach helps to solve the problem by eating the algae on plant leaves.

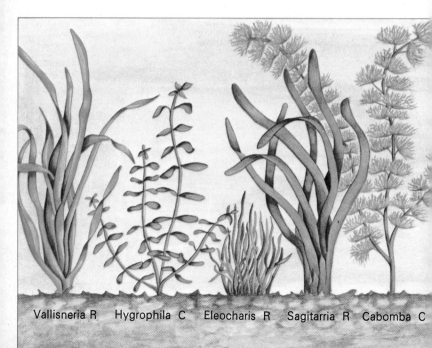

Vallisneria R   Hygrophila C   Eleocharis R   Sagitarria R   Cabomba C

Don't put too many different kinds of plants together since some only thrive at the expense of others. Arrange the plants in the tank away from the front so that you can see in. A 60cm x 30cm x 38cm tank will need no more than 30 plants. Here is a selection which will grow well together in a tropical tank: ten Vallisneria, six Cabomba, six Hygrophila, three Cryptocorynes, three Bacopa, one Echinodorus. Don't fill the tank too full of plants to start with – they soon grow larger.

Plants that are grown from cuttings (C) should be planted in small bunches.

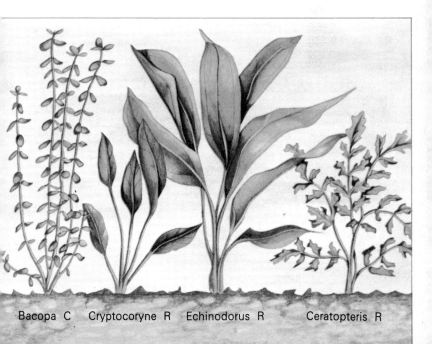

Bacopa C   Cryptocoryne R   Echinodorus R   Ceratopteris R

Coldwater aquaria

When putting any new fish into a tank, the temperature of the water in the plastic bag and in the tank must be the same. Float the bag in the tank for a few minutes. Then let the fish out gently.

All coldwater fish need lots of oxygen and swimming space so be careful not to overcrowd your tank. Make sure the water temperature stays as even as possible by keeping the tank out of the sun in a cool spot.

Goldfish are the most popular coldwater fish. There are many varieties – some beautiful, others rather bizarre. Common Goldfish are very hardy and easy to keep. You can even keep them outside. Fancy ones are smaller and are best kept indoors.

Sunfish are easy to keep though they may refuse dried food. They are peaceful enough to be kept with other short-finned fish, although it is better to keep them alone. They grow to about 10cm long. Bitterling may reach 8cm long. They can be kept in large tanks but are a bit shy, so may hide.

Never pick coldwater fish up in your hand. It can damage their scales and fins. Always use a net to catch and hold them.

Male Sunfish dig a hollow for the eggs with their fins.

They spawn over the hollow and the eggs stick to the bottom.

The male guards the eggs and cares for the young when they hatch.

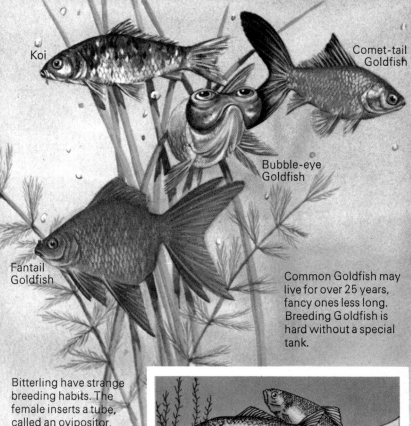

Koi

Comet-tail
Goldfish

Bubble-eye
Goldfish

Fantail
Goldfish

Common Goldfish may live for over 25 years, fancy ones less long. Breeding Goldfish is hard without a special tank.

Bitterling have strange breeding habits. The female inserts a tube, called an ovipositor, into the shell of a freshwater mussel. She lays her eggs through the tube. The mussel shelters them till they hatch. It is very hard to breed Bitterling in aquaria ; only experts try to do it.

13

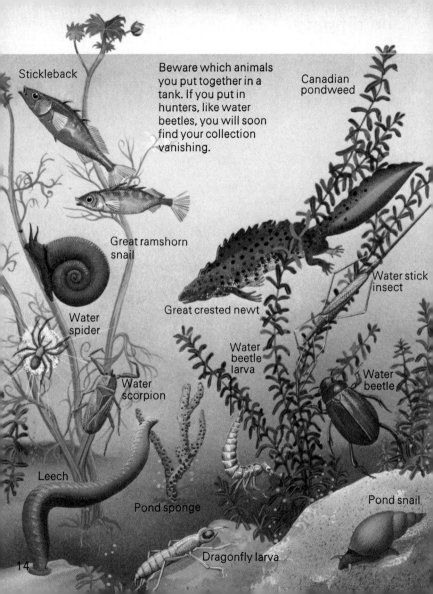

Stickleback

Beware which animals you put together in a tank. If you put in hunters, like water beetles, you will soon find your collection vanishing.

Canadian pondweed

Great ramshorn snail

Water stick insect

Great crested newt

Water spider

Water beetle larva

Water beetle

Water scorpion

Leech

Pond sponge

Pond snail

Dragonfly larva

14

Pond dipping

Instead of buying coldwater fish you could try catching some from ponds and streams. Use nets, not lines, because the hooks damage the fish and reduce their chances of survival. Many wild fish never feel at home in an aquarium. Your best chance of success is with small, young ones.

Sticklebacks (or tiddlers) make good pet fish, but they are aggressive. They terrorise fish bigger than themselves, so keep them with their own kind. The males turn lovely colours at breeding time.

If you don't have a tank try keeping pond creatures in jars full of water. You need a net to catch them and plastic bags to take them home. Clumps of water plants are rich hunting grounds. Plunge in your net or pull out some weed and shake it; it's amazing what drops out. Don't forget to look under stones. A netful of mud may hold many interesting specimens too.

Pond creatures will live happily in a 2 lb jam jar holding some 10cm of water at most. Give them a sprig of water plant to climb on or hide in.

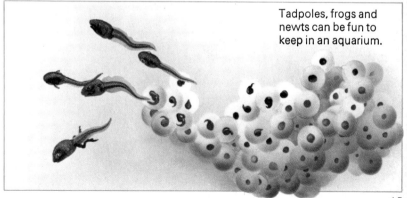

Tadpoles, frogs and newts can be fun to keep in an aquarium.

The tropical tank

The choice of tropical fish is enormous. A beginner should seek advice before buying any. At first, choose fish that are hardy, easy to care for and cheap. The cheaper ones are usually the hardiest and most suitable for beginners. Always buy young healthy ones. Find out about the needs of your fish. Are they happy in small shoals, or do they prefer to be on their own?

Here is a good selection of small fish that you might put in a 60cm x 30cm x 38cm tropical tank : six Neon Tetras or Cardinal Tetras, two Zebra Danios, four Harlequins, two Cherry Barbs, two Checker Barbs, two Kuhli Eels, two Pencil Fish, two Platies, two Bloodfins, a Corydoras Catfish and a Sucking Loach – a total of 26 fish.

If you want a community tank – one with many different kinds of fish in it – you must choose peaceful species, not ones that can only be kept with their own kind. Buy fish of roughly the same size to discourage them from bullying each other. An aggressive one will torment the others. If you want to mix bigger fish with smaller ones they must be very peaceful types.

If you want bigger fish in your tank here is a possible selection: two Rosy or Nigger Barbs, two Black Mollies, two Leeri Gouramis, two Blind Cave Fish, two Corydoras Catfish, a Sucking Catfish, a Red Tailed Black Shark, two Thick Lip Gouramis and two Pearl or Giant Danios – 16 fish in all. You can of course put more small fish together than big ones.

In the tank are:
1. Zebra Danios
2. Neon Tetras
3. Red Platies
4. Pencil Fish
5. Corydoras Catfish
6. Cherry Barbs
7. Kuhli Eel
8. Harlequin Fish

17

Livebearers

Unlike other fish, livebearers give birth to tiny young called 'fry', instead of laying eggs. Guppies, Mollies, Swordtails and Platies are all livebearers. They are good fish for beginners to keep because most of them are hardy, easy to look after and thrive in a community tank. Platies are ideal. There are lots of different coloured varieties to choose from and they live very happily in a community. Of the Mollies, the Black Molly is one of the most striking and easiest to look after.

A Guppy gives birth to her young (above). When you are breeding livebearers, especially in a community tank, give your fish plenty of live food. This will discourage them from eating the newborn fry.

Male Fantail Guppy

Black Mollies

Livebearers breed easily, even in community tanks, and have many young. Guppies are known as 'Million Fish' because they have so many. Females can give birth every five or six weeks to as many as a hundred young. Not all survive because the parents and other fish eat them.

To breed livebearers properly you need a separate tank so you can remove the parents as soon as the fry are born. In a community tank, the fry will need thick clumps of plants to hide in.

Blue Platies

Sailfin Molly

Platies are smaller than Swordtails but are closely related. Crossbreeding sometimes takes place. Swordtails and Mollies can grow to 7cms (not counting their tails) They can be kept with bigger fish.

Male Red Swordtail

Pair of Green Swordtails

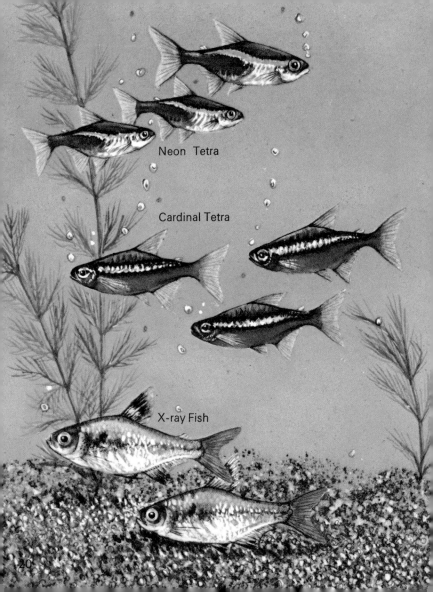

Neon Tetra

Cardinal Tetra

X-ray Fish

Characins

Most Characins come from South America but a few are from Africa. The brilliant colours of many of these lovely fish help them find each other in murky rivers.

Tetras, a kind of Characin, make good pet fish. They live best in small shoals of four to six. They like plenty of plants in the tank to give them some natural shelter. When buying Tetras get well grown specimens. They are sometimes sold as small as 1cm long, but at this size other fish tend to look on them as tasty snacks! Neon Tetras are commoner and cheaper than the more brilliant Cardinal Tetras.

The bigger, though peaceful, Blind Cave Fish is most unusual. Eyes are useless in the pitch dark underground streams of Mexico where it comes from, and so, over many generations, they have disappeared. This fish relies on other senses to find its food and mate.

The famous Piranha Fish would soon wipe out your collection if kept in a community tank.. They eat even their own kind and wouldn't say no to your finger!

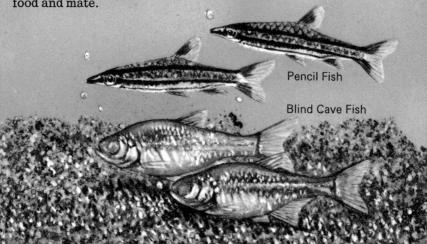

Pencil Fish

Blind Cave Fish

The carp family

Goldfish are the best known members of this family but there are many beautiful tropical carp too. These are good beginners' fish as they are hardy and live happily in community tanks. It is fun to keep them as they are livelier than most other fish.

Barbs, Danios and Rasboras all belong to the carp family. They are boisterous little fish, often the clowns of the aquarium. They are constantly darting about, so give them plenty of space to swim in. The back and sides of the tank should be densely planted. All carp are sociable and are happiest in shoals. Alone, they tend to hide away sadly among the plants.

Their tank should have an aerator – these fish need lots of oxygen because they are so active. They also have big appetites. But don't give them more than they can eat in three minutes or the tank may become polluted by left-over food.

White Cloud Mountain Minnows (above) are very small so don't put them with much bigger fish or you may lose them.

Rasboras and Danios prefer to stay near the surface. They like a clear space to dart around in. Danios, especially Giant Danios, are good jumpers so be sure there's a cover on your tank. Zebra Danios are very easy to breed, but if not stopped they will eat their own eggs.

22

Harlequin Fish

Most Barbs are fine in a community tank, although Tiger Barbs may bully the other fish. Don't put them in with smaller varieties.

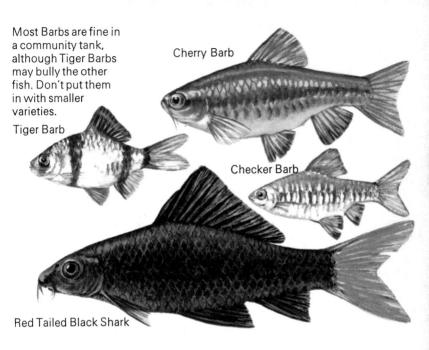

Cherry Barb

Tiger Barb

Checker Barb

Red Tailed Black Shark

Zebra Danios

Keep adult Angel
Fish (Cichlids)
with their own kind —
they may eat smaller
companions. Their long
fins also tempt fin-
nippers, like Tiger Barbs.

Cichlids and Labyrinths

Cichlids are poor community fish. They are usually large and quarrelsome and they uproot plants. But in a tank on their own they can be fun to keep. They are easy to breed and make good parents.

Dwarf Cichlids are smaller but they too can be aggressive. You can keep them in pairs in a community tank, but give them plenty of hiding places among the rocks and plants.

Although you usually buy them when they are small, Angel Fish grow quite big. They are not suitable for community tanks – you cannot trust them not to eat small fish.

Labyrinths can take oxygen from the air as well as from water so they can survive in poorly aerated water. Paradise Fish, Gouramis and Siamese Fighting Fish are all Labyrinths. Many make poor community fish because they are aggressive.

Male Siamese Fighting Fish

Siamese Fighting Fish are not good in community tanks. They can be aggressive and are also easy prey for fin-nippers. Keep one male and a few females; never put two males together or they will fight.

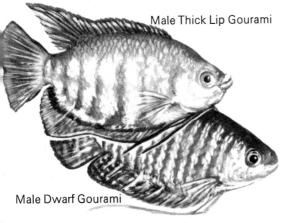

Male Thick Lip Gourami

Male Dwarf Gourami

Many Gouramis are better kept with others of their kind. But some, like the Thick Lip and Dwarf Gouramis (left), will live peacefully in a community tank. They are shy and need plenty of places to hide so make sure the tank has enough plants and rocks.

25

Most Catfish and Eels (below) tend to be more active at night so you may not see much of them during the day.

Albino Corydoras Catfish

Sucker-mouthed Catfish

Kuhli Eel

26

Catfish and Loaches

Catfish and Loaches may not be as colourful as their brilliant companions, but they make up for it in character and usefulness.

Most Corydoras Catfish are scavengers. They love rooting in gravel with their pointed mouths looking for food. If you spill a little food in the tank by accident, your Catfish will oblige by clearing it up for you. But if they can't find enough to eat on the bottom they will join the other fish feeding higher up the tank.

Sucking Catfish and Sucking Loaches are useful for clearing the tank of algae. If there isn't enough for them to live on you may have to feed them tiny bits of boiled spinach or lettuce as well. Sucking Catfish get along well with other species but badly with each other. Only keep one in a small tank. You can put more in a large tank so long as there are plenty of hiding places.

Loaches and Catfish eat algae growing on plants but you still need a scraper to clear it off the tank walls.

Daily jobs
Check all is well with the fish and the plants. Remove any dead fish or plants at once. Feed fish – but only a little at a time. If you accidentally give too much food, remove it at once with a siphon or dip tube.

Weekly jobs
Clean the tank sides and siphon off debris. Cut dead leaves off the plants. Clean out the mechanical filter system thoroughly and other equipment as it becomes necessary. Top up the water.

Monthly jobs
Draw off a quarter of the water in the tank. Replace it with fresh water at the same temperature. Thin out the plants that are growing too dense. Loosen the gravel with a small stick.

Fish care

Buy a dispenser for feeding tubifex worms to your fish. Otherwise the worms will hide in the gravel before the fish can eat them.

Once your tank is stocked with fish you must know how to care for them. The most important rule is '*Don't overfeed*'. You can feed fish several times a day but never give them more food than they can finish in three minutes. Extra food rots and pollutes the water. Many more fish are killed by polluted water than by starvation. If you are going away leave your fish unfed rather than allow an inexperienced person to feed them. They can survive up to three weeks without eating.

Buy specially prepared dried flake food from pet shops. Now and then give them live food, such as gnat larvae, daphnia and tubifex worms, which you can also buy. Some fish, like Mollies, need plant food to keep them in peak condition. Give them tiny pieces of boiled spinach or crushed up lettuce.

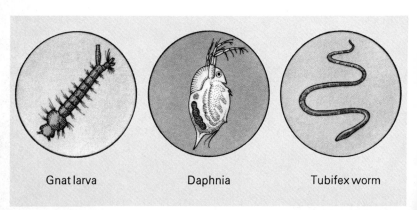

Gnat larva   Daphnia   Tubifex worm

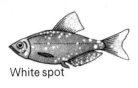

White spot

Velvet

Fin rot

Boils

Many fish diseases are caused by poor tank conditions. Overcrowding, wrong or suddenly changed water temperature, water pollution and overfeeding are usually the causes. If something is wrong with your fish, check tank conditions. An improvement in these may quickly put the fish right. Replacing a third of the tank water may help the fish to recover more quickly.

Signs of illness to look for are drooping, loss of colour, fins clamped up tightly and shimmying (irregular jerky movements). Very small white spots on the fins – White Spot Disease – is sometimes found on newly-bought fish.

When you have one sick fish, it is sometimes kindest to kill it so it does not infect the others. But many common diseases (left) can be cured if treated promptly with antiseptic solutions from a pet shop.

Of the two Harlequins (right) one is sick and one healthy. The sick one holds its fins close to its side and is gasping for air at the surface. The other keeps its fins erect and breathes easily. It looks bright and alert.

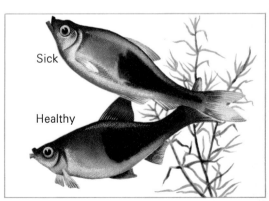

Sick

Healthy

Breeding

Breeding fish is fascinating but it can be difficult. Some have very strange breeding habits and most need separate tanks to breed successfully. In these, the temperature should be slightly higher than normal. Livebearers are among the easiest to breed and will do so even in a community tank.

Before you try to breed, find out all about the habits and needs of your fish. Some, like the Barbs, scatter their eggs. They tend to eat their spawn and so must be separated from it immediately. Others, like the Cichlids, lay their eggs on plant leaves or rocks. They are good parents and should be left with their young. Male Siamese Fighting Fish are careful fathers, but remove the female after spawning or else the male will kill her.

It is often hard to tell males and females apart. Rather than match-making, it is best to let fish choose their own partners.

Spraying Characins lay eggs out of the water. They leap out together to spawn on a leaf then slip back into the water.

The male Siamese Fighting Fish builds a nest of bubbles for the eggs. He looks after them until the fry hatch.

Firemouth Cichlids breed easily if they have a special tank to themselves. Both parents guard the fry.

Guppies (below) are very fertile livebearers. Zebra Danios (right) are egg scatterers. Both eat their young if given the chance.

Hooked on fish

Once you have taken the plunge and begun to keep fish, you will find it is an endlessly fascinating hobby. With practice you will soon be rearing better specimens. You may wish to display them at shows and competitions run by aquarium societies. You could start to collect different varieties or else just specialise in one kind. You may even decide to keep rare and difficult kinds, like the beautiful Discus.

Some people enjoy keeping odd-looking varieties. A few, such as Mudskippers, Pufferfish and Elephant-nose Fish, don't look much like fish at all.

As you gain experience with fish, you may start to collect them in ever greater numbers. Then you will need more tanks. Some people give whole rooms over to their aquaria. At that stage, you will find yourself spending a huge amount of time enjoying your fish.

Firemouth Cichlids